T0004611

THE
BOOK OF
LANGUAGES

Talk your way
around the world

Mick Webb

Owlkids Books

Text © 2013 Franklin Watts

Published in North America in 2015 by Owlkids Books Inc.
First printing in paperback, 2020

Published in the UK under the title *The Book of Languages: Speak Your Way Around the World* in 2013 by Franklin Watts (a division of Hachette Children's Books, an Hachette UK Company)

Quechua language section created by Owlkids Books.

Picture credits: Achindivers/Shutterstock: 58b. AF archive/Alamy: 9b. art4all/Shutterstock: 7t. © Warangkana Charuyodhin/Dreamstime: 55b. Countrystylephotography/istockphoto: 59b. Craig Dingle/istockphoto: 59c. Arnold Lorrie Hicks/Corbis: 54c. jayfish/shutterstock: 57c. Earle Keatley/istockphoto: 59t. Laralova/shutterstock: 57b. ollyy/Shutterstock: 54b. Shako/Shutterstock: 56. Shutterstock: all flags. Supri Suharjoto/Shutterstock: 9t. Peter Waters/Shutterstock: 58c. World History Archive/Alamy: 7b.

Every attempt has been made to clear copyright. Should there be any inadvertent omission please apply to the publisher for rectification.

All rights reserved. No part of this publication may be reproduced, stored in a retrieval system, or transmitted in any form or by any means, without the prior written permission of Owlkids Books Inc., or in the case of photocopying or other reprographic copying, a license from the Canadian Copyright Licensing Agency (Access Copyright). For an Access Copyright license, visit www.accesscopyright.ca or call toll-free to 1-800-893-5777.

Owlkids Books acknowledges the financial support of the Canada Council for the Arts, the Ontario Arts Council, the Government of Canada through the Canada Book Fund (CBF) and the Government of Ontario through the Ontario Creates Book Initiative for our publishing activities.

Owlkids Books gratefully acknowledges that our office in Toronto is located on the traditional territory of many nations, including the Mississaugas of the Credit, the Chippewa, the Wendat, the Anishinaabeg, and the Haudenosaunee Peoples.

Published in Canada by Owlkids Books Inc., 1 Eglinton Avenue East, Toronto, ON M4P 3A1
Published in the US by Owlkids Books Inc., 1700 Fourth Street, Berkeley, CA 94710

Library and Archives Canada Cataloguing in Publication

Title: The book of languages : talk your way around the world / Mick Webb.
Names: Webb, Mick, author.
Description: Reprint. Previously published: Toronto: Owlkids Books Inc., 2015. | Includes index.
Identifiers: Canadiana 20190236507 | ISBN 9781771474245 (softcover)
Subjects: LCSH: Language and languages—Juvenile literature.
Classification: LCC P107 .W43 2020 | DDC j400—dc23

Library of Congress Control Number: 2014950141

MIX
Paper from responsible sources
FSC® C016245
www.fsc.org

Manufactured in Manitoba, Canada, by Friesens, in July 2023
Job #299228

D   E   F   G   H   I

ONTARIO ARTS COUNCIL
CONSEIL DES ARTS DE L'ONTARIO
an Ontario government agency
un organisme du gouvernement de l'Ontario

Canada Council for the Arts   Conseil des Arts du Canada

Canadä

Publisher of Chirp, Chickadee and OWL
www.owlkidsbooks.com

Owlkids Books is a division of   bayard canada

Contents

Say "Hello" in 48

Aang
Aleut-Eskimo

Ullukkut
Inuktitut

Hej
Danish

Hello
English

Hallo
Dutch

Tanisi
Cree

Kuei
Innu

Helo
Welsh

Bonjour
French

Hau
Lakota

Kaixo
Basque

Boozhoo
Anishinabe

Yáʼatʼééh
Navajo

Kwe'
Mi'kmaq

Hola
Spanish

Buongiorno
Italian

Halito
Choctaw

Niltse
Nahuatl

Alo
Haitian Creole

Sakaric
K'iche'

Olá
Portuguese

Walale
Umbundu

Rimaykullayki
Quechua

Hallo
Afrikaans

Mbaé'ch'tpa
Guaraní

Hello!

4

different languages

Hei
Finnish

Guten Tag
German

Cześć
Polish

Szia
Hungarian

Zdravstvujtye
Russian

Sain baina uu
Mongolian

Merhaba
Turkish

Konnichiwa
Japanese

Shalom
Hebrew

Salaam
Iranian

Nǐ hǎo
Mandarin

Annyeong haseyo
Korean

Yassou
Greek

dravo
oatian

Marhaba
Arabic

Sawàt-dii
Thai

Selamat pagi
Malay

Jambo
Swahili

Namaste
Hindi-Urdu

Nomaashkaar
Bengali

Kaya
Noongar

Kia ora
Maori

Sawubona
Zulu

Why language is important

One of the most important differences between human beings and other animals is our use of language. Language allows us to tell other people what we want, what we think, and what we feel, and also understand what others are saying to us.

Nearly 7,000 languages are spoken in the world. Some languages have many millions of speakers, whereas some may have fewer than ten. All of these languages do the same thing: allow us to communicate with others. We all need to greet people, say who we are, tell stories and jokes, discuss and persuade, even let off steam if we hit our thumb with a hammer. To do these things we need language.

¿Qué?

You what?

In this book...

• This book looks at 21 of the world's languages. You can find out about their history and where they are spoken. You can see what they look like and also learn to speak a few words and phrases (pages 12–53).

• Despite their differences, languages are related, like humans. You can find out about the different language families on pages 10–11.

• Language is so important to us that we have created ways to communicate even when we cannot speak or hear. On pages 54–57 you can find out about some non-verbal languages.

Scripts and pronunciation

Not all languages are written in the same way. The written forms are called scripts. Chinese can be written using characters, like tiny paintings: 鴶儈. Russian script uses the Cyrillic alphabet, with letters like this: Ж. English and lots of other languages use the Latin alphabet (**A**, **B**, **C**, etc.). In this book we have changed all the words into the Latin script so you can read them more easily. This is called "transcription." The alphabets for each language, with the names of the letters, are shown on the side of the right-hand pages. To make reading as easy as possible, we have used the most simplified transcriptions and also written the alphabets of all languages from left to right. You'll also find short pronunciation guides that describe the way that letters sound when they are spoken.

A short history of language

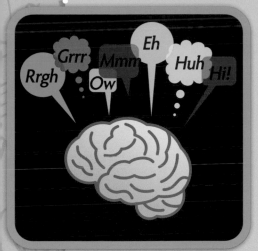

No one knows exactly when or how humans first began to speak. At some point, between 100,000 and 50,000 years ago, the brains of our prehistoric ancestors changed. This made us able to use language rather than just grunt like other apes. We don't know whether this ability appeared suddenly or developed gradually over thousands of years. Now every child is able to learn his or her own native language (called a mother tongue), as well as the languages spoken by others.

Languages travel

Separate languages grew up in different places and have traveled with the people who speak them. This has happened through trade, migration and war. For example, when the Anglo-Saxons invaded Britain in the 5th century, they brought their own language with them and it became the basis of English. The German language grew up in the region which the Anglo-Saxons came from, and so English and German have some similarities. They are part of the same language family. (See page 10.)

Languages RIP

Languages can die out and become extinct, just like species of animals. This happens when the children stop learning their parents' language because another language is more useful. When there is no one left to speak a language it is considered "dead." Of the 7,000 languages spoken in the world today, half are at risk of dying out. There are some 200 languages that are critically endangered with fewer than ten speakers. On the other hand, we are still discovering unique languages in remote places like the Amazon rain forest.

The oldest language

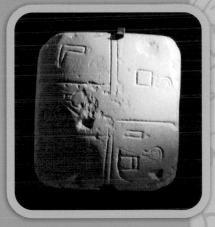

The oldest language still being spoken today is thought to be Tamil. According to recent archaeological evidence, Tamil was spoken in southern India more than 5,000 years ago.

However, the first written words were probably in the ancient language used by the Sumerian people. They lived in Mesopotamia, which is now the country of Iraq. Their script was found on the Kish tablet (above). It has been dated to 3,500 BC.

Language facts

The most spoken language

The most widely spoken language in the world is Mandarin Chinese, which has over a billion speakers. This is based on the number of people who use it as their first language or mother tongue. It is followed by Hindi-Urdu, Spanish and English.

普通話

The least spoken language

Lots of languages are spoken by just a handful of people. Deep in the Amazon rain forest, on the Brazilian border with Bolivia, Guarasu has just two speakers.

Latin

Although Latin is considered a dead language, there are Latin phrases that are still used a lot today. Lawyers speak of **prima facie** evidence, which is Latin for "at first sight." You'll also hear people say **gratis** (free), **persona non grata** (someone who's not welcome) and **et cetera** (and other things), written as "etc."

New languages

Languages are still being discovered. In 2010, researchers learned about a unique language in India. It is called Koro and is spoken by farming people in the Indian state of Arunachal Pradesh, near the borders with China, Tibet and Burma.

Official languages

A country's official language is the language that is used within government, which includes courts of law and public administration. A country can have more than one language as its official language. For example, English, Maori and New Zealand Sign Language are all official languages in New Zealand.

Invented languages

There have been many attempts to invent a world language that everyone can learn to speak. The best known is Esperanto. It was created in the 1870s by a Polish doctor, Ludwig Zamenhof. His language was based on a mixture of European languages. The vocabulary comes mainly from Romance languages such as Italian and Spanish. The Esperanto for "I speak Esperanto" is **"Mi parolas Esperanton."**

Textese

Textese is a new way of writing languages, often used when texting on a cell phone. In English, it abbreviates words, uses digits like "2" and "4" to replace words, and creates acronyms where initial letters can stand for a complete phrase:
LOL = laugh out loud.

Elvish

The author J.R.R. Tolkien created a number of Elvish languages for the elves in his book *The Lord of the Rings*. The best-known is Quenya. It was based on Finnish, the language of Finland.

Pidgin

Pidgin language is a simplified language used by people who do not have a language in common. Chinese pidgin English was invented by traders in the 17th–19th centuries. It has given us some well-known phrases, like **"no-go,"** **"no-can-do"** and **"look-see."**

Klingon

The Klingon language was invented by Marc Okrand for the 1984 film *Star Trek 3*. "Do you speak Klingon?" is **"tlhIngan Hol Dojatlh'a?"**

Slang

Slang is a kind of language that is not considered standard or proper. It changes very quickly and is often used by young people. "Back slang" uses words spoken backwards and has been used by prison inmates who want to communicate without being understood by their guards. **Yob** ("boy" spelled backwards) is an example, now commonly used in Britain.

Language families

Like people, languages belong to different families. Languages in the same family have connections with each other. They share a common ancestor and may have similar features.

The map below shows you where the main language families are spoken.

- ■ Afro-Asiatic
- ■ Altaic
- ■ Austro-Asiatic
- ■ Austronesian
- ■ Dravidian
- ■ Indo-European
- ■ Japonic
- ■ Niger-Congo
- ■ Sino-Tibetan
- ■ Tai Kadai
- ■ Uralic

A language family tree

The larger language families have their own family trees, which are split into smaller groups of languages, called branches. Here you can see how one of these language families, Indo-European, breaks off into different languages. How many of these have you heard of?

INDO-EUROPEAN LANGUAGE TREE

Language families

There are 110 separate language families. Below you can see a breakdown of the main ones.

Indo-European

Spoken by **46%** of the world's population. This is the largest language family and includes languages spoken across Europe, the Americas and parts of Asia. It's spoken by **3 billion people** and includes languages such as English, Welsh, Russian, Hindi-Urdu and Spanish.

Niger-Congo

Spoken by **6.4%** of the world's population. This family has more than 1,300 languages. They are spoken in the southern half of Africa. The most widely spoken is Swahili.

Austronesian

Spoken by **5.9%** of the world's population. These languages are found in the countries around the Pacific Ocean. The most widely spoken is Malay.

Altaic

Spoken by **2.3%** of the world's population. This family spreads through central and northern Asia. It includes Turkish and Mongolian. Some linguists also put Korean and Japanese in this family. If you include them, this family is spoken by **4.4%** of the world's population.

Other language families

Japonic, which may include Japanese and Korean. **Austro-Asiatic,** which includes Vietnamese and Khmer, the official languages of Vietnam and Cambodia. **Tai Kadai,** which includes the main languages of Thailand and Laos. **Uralic,** which includes Hungarian, Finnish and Estonian. **Language isolates:** languages which have no obvious connection with any other language, such as Basque.

Dravidian

Spoken by **3.7%** of the world's population. The languages in this family are found mainly in southern India and Sri Lanka. The best known is Tamil.

Afro-Asiatic

Spoken by **6.1%** of the world's population. These languages are found in the north of Africa and the Middle East. Arabic is the most widely spoken.

Sino-Tibetan

Spoken by **21%** of the world's population. This family of East Asian languages includes Mandarin Chinese.

8.6%

2.3%

3.7%

5.9%

6.1%

6.4%

21%

46%

80

70

60

50

40

30

20

10

0

Arabic-speaking countries

Can you find them on the map?

 Algeria (3)

 Bahrain (18)

 Egypt (6)

 Eritrea (8)

 Iraq (13)

 Jordan (16)

 Kuwait (17)

 Lebanon (15)

 Libya (5)

 Mauritania (1)

 Morocco (2)

 Oman (11)

 Qatar (19)

 Saudi Arabia (12)

 Somalia (9)

 Sudan (7)

 Syria (14)

 Tunisia (4)

 UEA (20)

 Yemen (10)

العربية
(Al-'Arabiyah)

Arabic

A short history of Arabic

Arabic is spoken throughout the Middle East and the northern part of Africa. Classical Arabic developed in the 7th century. It was the language in which the Koran, the holy text of the Islamic religion, was written. Called *Qu'ran* in Arabic, it helped to spread the Arabic language to the areas where it is now spoken.

There is one kind of written Arabic used in the Arabic-speaking world, called Modern Standard Arabic.

There are many different versions of spoken Arabic, called dialects. Egyptian Arabic is the most widely understood, due to the number of films made in Egypt and shown in other Arabic states.

Where is it spoken?

Arabic is the first language of well over **200 million people**. It is also the religious language of more than a billion Muslims across the world.

Greetings

Marhaba	Hello
Ila al'likaa'	Goodbye
Ana ismee...	My name is…
Kaifa haluki?	How are you? (to a female)
Kaifa haluka?	How are you? (to a male)
Ana bikhair, shukran	I'm fine, thank you
Lastoo bikhair	I'm not well

Numbers

1	waahid	6	sitta
2	eeth-nayn	7	sab'a
3	thalaatha	8	thamaaneeya
4	arba'a	9	tis'a
5	khamsa	10	asharra

Pronunciation points

Arabic vowels can have different sounds

a in **ana** sounds like the "a" sound in "bad"

aa in **waahid** sounds like the "a" in "father"

ay in **eeth nayn** sounds like "ai" in "paid"

Some Arabic consonants are pronounced at the back of your throat:

kh in **bikhair** has a raspy sound like "ch" in the Scottish word "loch"

h in **haluka** is like the sound of an "h" while blowing on a mirror to clean it

' The apostrophe in a word like **sab'a** is like the short pause in the middle of "uh-oh"

Speak Arabic!

Marhaba, kaifa haluka?
Hello, how are you?

Ana bikhair, shukran
I'm fine, thanks

Ana ismee Ali. Maa ismuka?
My name is Ali. What are you called?

Ana ismee Peter. Araka ghadan
I'm Peter. See you later

Azeem! Ila al'likaa'
Great! Goodbye

Language matters

Arabic is written and read from right to left. Readers of Arabic books begin from what English speakers think of as the end of the book.

The Arabic alphabet has 28 letters, only three of which are vowels. This is because vowels are often left out in written Arabic. They are shown by marks (like accents) above or below the letters.

alif ba taa tha jim haa kha dal dhal ra zay sin shin sad dad ta za ayn ghayn fa qaf kaf lam mim nuun ha waw ya

13

עִבְרִית
(Ivrit)

Hebrew

Hebrew-speaking countries

⬚ Israel

A short history of Hebrew

The original Hebrew language is called Classical or Biblical Hebrew because it was the main language in which the Bible was written.

By around 500 BC, Hebrew was no longer spoken and was only used in religious writing. At the end of the 19th century, when Jews began to settle again in Palestine, Hebrew was reintroduced as a language that could be used for everyday purposes. This was called Modern Hebrew.

Along with Arabic, it is one of the two official languages of the state of Israel. There are similarities between the sounds of words in Hebrew and Arabic, although they have completely different alphabets.

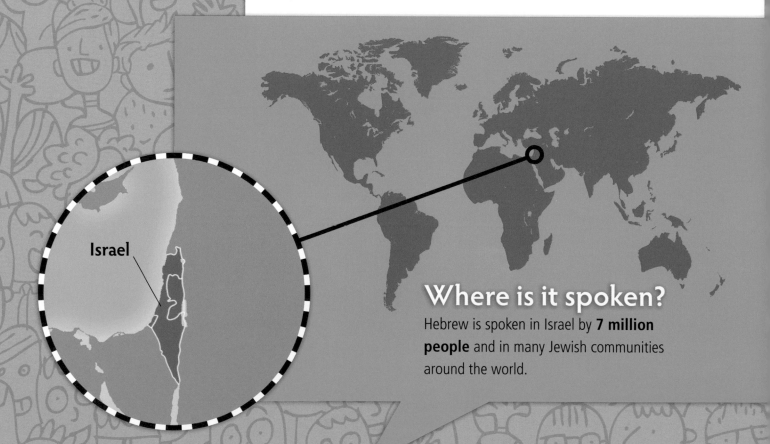

Israel

Where is it spoken?

Hebrew is spoken in Israel by **7 million people** and in many Jewish communities around the world.

Greetings

Shalom	Hello/Goodbye
Shmi…	My name is…
Ma shlomech?	How are you? (to a female)
Ma shlomcha?	How are you? (to a male)
B'seder, todah	I'm fine, thank you
Lo tov	Not so good!

Numbers

There are two words for each number. The first one is for counting masculine words. The second is for counting feminine words.

1 **echad; achat**

2 **shnayim; shtayim**

3 **shlosha; shalosh**

4 **arba'a; arba**

5 **chamisha; chames**

6 **shisha; shes**

7 **shva'a; sheva**

8 **shmona; shmone**

9 **tish'a; tesha**

10 **asara; eser**

Pronunciation points

ch in **shomlech** sounds like an "h" pronounced at the back of the throat

r in **lehitraot** is also pronounced at the back of your throat, like a French "r"

i sounds like "ee" in "feed"

e sounds like "e" in "get"

o sounds like "o" in "toe"

a sounds like "a" in "mat"

u sounds like "oo" in "cool"

Speak Hebrew!

Shalom, ma shlomech? — Hello, how are you?

B'seder, todah — I'm fine, thanks

Shmi Livna. Eich korim lach? — My name is Liv. What are you called?

Shmi Jane. Lehitraot — I'm Jane. See you later

Al magniv! Shalom — Great! Goodbye

Language matters

Hebrew is written from right to left, like Arabic. It is written in squared-off letters. The letters are not joined up in Hebrew words but are written separately. Vowels are not usually written down at all, though they can be marked with a series of dots and dashes. Three small dots under a letter show an "e" sound.

alef bet gimel dalet he vav zayin chet tet yod kaf lamed mem nun samech ayin peh tsadi kof resh sheen tav kaf mem nun peh tsadi soft soft soft soft soft soft soft

日本語
(Nihongo)

Japanese

Japanese-speaking countries

● Japan

A short history of Japanese

The first script for writing Japanese used Chinese characters. Called Kanji, it was imported into Japan in the 5th century. Kanji is still used, alongside two other alphabets (Hiragana and Katakana), for writing Japanese.

For nearly a hundred years, until the end of the Second World War (1939–45), Japan's empire included Malaysia, Indonesia and Singapore. Japanese was an official language in these countries. Nowadays, as well as the 125 million speakers in Japan, there are large communities of Japanese speakers who have migrated, particularly to Brazil and the USA.

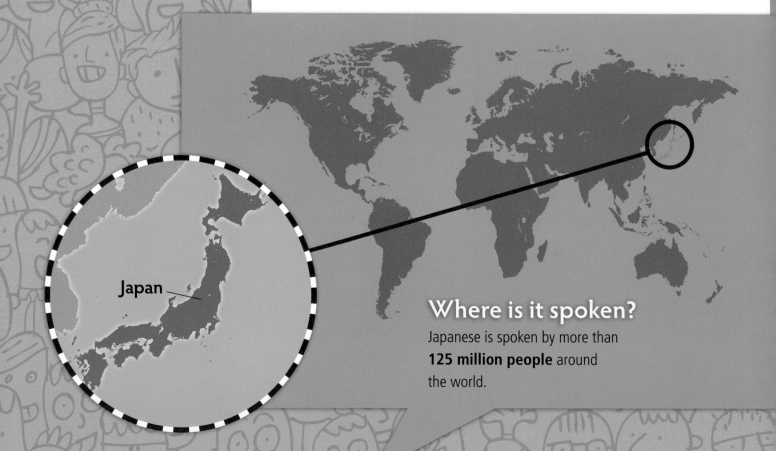

Japan

Where is it spoken?
Japanese is spoken by more than **125 million people** around the world.

Greetings

Konnichiwa	Hello
Sayonara	Goodbye
Watashi no namae wa…desu	My name is…
Ogenki desu ka?	How are you?
Genki ni shiteimasu	I'm fine, thank you
Genki ja arimasen	I'm not well

Numbers

1	ichi	6	roku
2	ni	7	shichi
3	san	8	hachi
4	shi	9	kyuu
5	go	10	juu

Pronunciation points

r in a word like **roku** is not like the English "r." It sounds more like an "l."

ts in a word like **tsunami** needs to be pronounced as one sound, with the tip of your tongue against the back of your top front teeth

a in a word like **san** sounds like "a" in "bar"

e sounds like "e" in "get"

i sounds like "ee" in "weed"

o sounds like "o" in "old"

u sounds like "oo" in "soon." However, at the end of a word like **desu**, you don't pronounce it at all.

Speak Japanese!

Konnichiwa, ogenki desu ka? — Hello, how are you?

Genki ni shiteimasu — I'm fine, thanks

Watashi no namae wa Aiko desu. Onamae wa nan desu ka? — My name is Aiko. What are you called?

Watashi no namae wa Mick desu. Atodene — I'm Mick. See you later

Sugoi! Sayonara — Great! Goodbye

Language matters

The Hiragana alphabet (shown here) has 46 symbols to represent all the syllables in spoken Japanese. There's also a way of writing Japanese in the Roman alphabet. It's called Romaji.

Japanese has lots of "loan words" called **gairaigo**. These are words from other languages that have become part of the Japanese language. They may also change, for example, "personal computer" is **paso kon**.

あ か さ た な は ま や ら わ ん
a ka sa ta na ha ma ya ra wa n

い き し ち に ひ み り　ゐ
i ki shi chi ni hi mi ri　u

う く す つ ぬ ふ む ゆ る　ゑ
u ku su tsu nu fu mu yu ru　e

え け せ て ね へ め　れ　を
e ke se te ne he me　re　o

お こ そ と の ほ も よ ろ を
o ko so to no ho mo yo ro wo

17

Türkçe

Turkish

Turkish-speaking countries

 Cyprus

Türkiye

A short history of Turkish

Turkish is part of the family of Turkic languages, which came originally from Central Asia. Turkish was written in Arabic script until 1928. This was the year when a law was passed, changing the writing system to the Latin alphabet.

Turkish is the official language of Türkiye and the northern half of the island of Cyprus. Many Turkish speakers have migrated to northern European countries, with the greatest number of them living in Germany. Some Turkish words are used in English, especially words for foods such as "yoghurt" and "sis kebab."

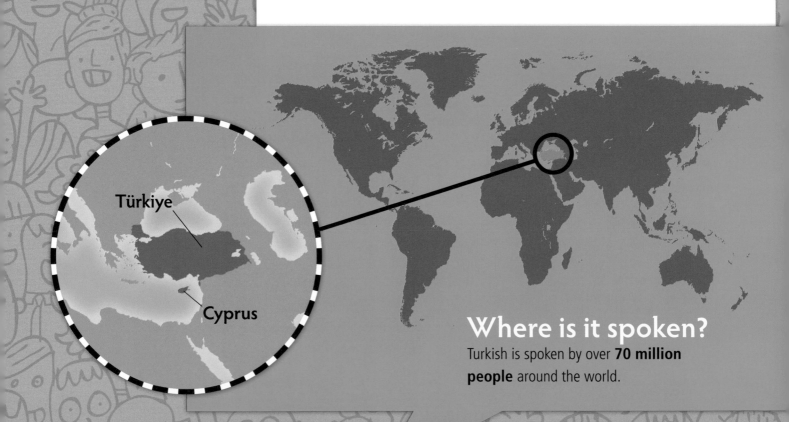

Türkiye

Cyprus

Where is it spoken?

Turkish is spoken by over **70 million people** around the world.

Greetings

Merhaba	Hello
Hoşçakalın	Goodbye
Benim adım...	My name is...
Nasılsınız?	How are you?
İyiyim, teşekkür ederim	I'm fine, thank you
İyi değilim	I'm not well

Numbers

1	bir	6	altı
2	iki	7	yedi
3	üç	8	sekiz
4	dört	9	dokuz
5	beş	10	on

Speak Turkish!

Merhaba. Nasılsınız? — Hello, how are you?

İyiyim, teşekkür ederim — I'm fine, thanks

Benim adım Leyla. Isminiz ne? — My name is Leyla. What are you called?

Benim adim Serena. Görüşürüz — I'm Serena. See you later

Harika! Hoşçakalin — Great! Goodbye

Pronunciation points

c	sounds like the "j" in "jam"
j	is a soft sound, like the "s" in "treasure"
ç	in **hoşçakalın** sounds like "ch" in "change"
ğ	in **değilim** is like "k" in "khaki"
ş	in the word **beş** is similar to the sound "sh" in "shell"
ö	in **dört** is similar to the "i" in "bird"
ü	in **üç** sounds like an "oo" with your lips pressed tightly together
i	sounds like "ee" in "meet," but ı (without a dot) in a word like **altı** sounds like "uh"

Language matters

There are two different words for "you." **Sen** is the informal, chatty word. **Siz** is the formal, polite one.

The verbs come at the end of sentences. The end of a Turkish verb tells you who or what the subject is, so you don't need a separate word for "I," "you," etc.

Turkish has borrowed words from many other languages. A large number have come from French. They are pronounced in a French way but spelled in a Turkish way. An example is **plaj** (beach), which comes from the French word **plage**.

Aa *a* Bb *b* Cc *ce* Çç *çe* Dd *de* Ee *e* Ff *fe* Gg *ge* Ğğ *yumuşak ge* Hh *he* Iı *ı* İi *i* Jj *je* Kk *k* Ll *le* Mm *me* Nn *ne* Oo *o* Öö *ö* Pp *pe* Rr *re* Ss *se* Şş *şe* Tt *te* Uu *u* Üü *ü* Vv *ve* Yy *ye* Zz *ze*

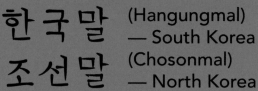

한국말 (Hangungmal)
— South Korea
조선말 (Chosonmal)
— North Korea

Korean

Korean-speaking countries

 North Korea
 South Korea

A short history of Korean

Until the 15th century, Korean had no writing system of its own. Chinese characters were used. In 1443, a new Korean script was invented by the Korean monarch, King Sejong. It's called Hangul in South Korea, but North Koreans know it as Chosongul.

Apart from the two countries where it is the official language, Korean is also spoken in large Korean communities in China, Japan, the USA and Central Asia. The name of the martial art Taekwondo is one of the few Korean words known internationally. In 2012, the South Korean singer PSY brought Korean to a wider audience with his song "Gangnam Style." It's been viewed by over a billion people on YouTube.

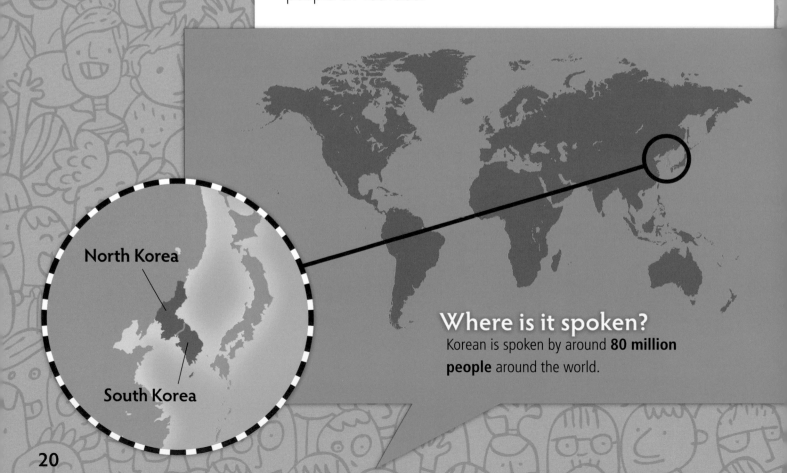

North Korea

South Korea

Where is it spoken?
Korean is spoken by around **80 million people** around the world.

Greetings

Annyeong haseyo	Hello
Annyeonghi gyeseyo	Goodbye (person leaving)
Annyeonghi gaseyo	Goodbye (person staying)
Jeoneun…imnida	My name is…
Eotteoke jinaesimnikka?	How are you?
Jal jinaemnida, gamsahamnida	Fine, thanks
Jeoneun apayo	I'm not well

Numbers

1	hana	6	yeoseot
2	dul	7	ilgop
3	set	8	yeodeol
4	net	9	ahop
5	daseot	10	yeol

Pronunciation points

a in **hana** is pronounced like "a" in the word "father"

o in **ahop** sounds like "o" in "pot"

eo in **annyeong** sounds like "o" in "low"

eu in **jeoneun** is a sound that doesn't exist in English. It's like a mixture of "oo" and "er"

ch in **choayo** sounds like the "tch" in "itch"

j in **jeoneun** sounds like "dg" in "badger"

ss in **haessoyo** is a very forceful way of pronouncing double "s"

Speak Korean!

Annyeong haseyo, eotteoke jinaesimnikka?	Hello, how are you?
Jal jinaemnida, gamsahamnida	I'm fine, thanks
Jeoneun Ji-hun imnida. Ireumi mwoeyo?	My name is Ji-hun. What are you called?
Jeoneun Alex imnida. Najunge bwayo	I'm Alex. See you later
Choayo! Annyeonghi gaseyo	Great! Goodbye

Language matters

The way that Korean is written is different from most other writing systems. The letters of the alphabet are not written one after another in a line. Instead, they are grouped together into syllables. For example, the name of the Korean script, Hangul, is not written as 하ㄴㄱㅡㄹ (h-a-n-g-u-l) but as 한글 (han-gul). The letters can have different sounds, depending on where they are in a word.

ㅢ uey
ㅞ wee
ㅙ way
ㅚ weh
ㅝ wuh
ㅘ wa
ㅖ wah
ㅒ yeh
ㅑ ya
ㅠ yew
ㅛ yo
ㅕ yaw yu
ㅐ e
ㅏ a
ㅣ uh
ㅗ o
ㅜ oo
ㅡ u
ㅎ ah
ㅍ h
ㅌ p
ㅋ t
ㅊ k
ㅉ ch
ㅈ jj
ㅅ j
ㅇ ng
ㅆ t,s
ㅂ s,t
ㅃ b
ㅁ p,b
ㄹ m
ㄷ l,r
ㄸ d
ㄴ t,d
ㄱ n
ㄲ g,k

English-speaking countries

Can you find them on the map?

 Australia (22)

 Antigua (8)

 Bahamas (4)

 Barbados (9)

 Belize (5)

 Bermuda (3)

 Canada (2)

 Cayman Islands (6)

 Gibraltar (14)

 Grenada (10)

 India (19)

 Ireland (12)

 Jamaica (7)

 Liberia (16)

 New Zealand (23)

 Philippines (21)

 Sierra Leone (15)

 Singapore (20)

 **South Africa** (17)

 Trinidad and Tobago (11)

 UK (13)

 USA (1)

 Zimbabwe (18)

English

A short history of English

English started as Anglo-Saxon — the language spoken by Angles, Saxons and Jutes, who crossed the English Channel from mainland Europe in the 5th century. After the invasion of William the Conqueror in 1066, Norman French became widely used and it was only in the 14th century that modern English emerged.

The invention of the printing press and translations of the Bible into English (the first in 1525) helped to spread the written language. The rule of the British Empire, from the 16th century, took the language across the world into countries as far apart as India, Canada and Barbados. Today, about two-thirds of the world's native speakers of English live in the USA.

Where is it spoken?

English is spoken as a first language by around **400 million people** around the world.

Greetings*

Hello, Hi	Hey
Goodbye	See you
My name is...	I am…
How are you?	How's it going?
I'm fine, thank you.	Great, thanks
Not so good!	Not great!

Numbers

1	one	6	six
2	two	7	seven
3	three	8	eight
4	four	9	nine
5	five	10	ten

Pronunciation points

English spelling is not a reliable guide to how you speak the language.

ou is a good example. There are four ways of pronouncing these two letters. They have a different sound in **thought**, **mouth**, **you** and **four**.

th (in **the**) is the English sound that is most unusual. It doesn't exist in many languages. People learning English as a second language find it difficult.

g as in **great**, has a hard sound. But when it is followed by an "e" (**Gemma**) or an "i" the sound can be soft, like j in **jam**.

c has a hard sound, like a "k," in a word like **called**. But it sounds like "s" when it is followed by "e" or "i" (**cease**).

* You already speak English, so here are some alternative ways to say our phrases. What others can you think of?

Speak English!*

Hello, how are you?	Hey, how's it going?
I'm fine, thanks	I'm good, thank you
My name is Gemma. What are you called?	I'm Gemma. Who are you?
I'm Wayne. See you tomorrow	I'm Wayne. Later!
Great! Goodbye!	Cool! Bye!

Language matters

English has simpler grammar than other languages in its language family. The verbs do not have as many endings. Also, nouns do not have genders and it's easy to make them plural. You usually just add an "s."

In common with other Germanic languages you can use an apostrophe to show that something belongs to someone. To say "Amanda's phone" in most languages, you need to say "the phone of Amanda."

The English spoken in North America has developed lots of alternative words to British English, such as **truck** instead of **lorry**, which have now become common in the English spoken around the world.

Aa a bee · Bb bee · Cc cee · Dd dee · Ee e · Ff ef · Gg gee · Hh aitch · Ii i · Jj jay · Kk kay · Ll el · Mm em · Nn en · Oo o · Pp pee · Qq cue · Rr ar · Ss ess · Tt tee · Uu u · Vv vee · Ww double-u · Xx ex · Yy wy · Zz zed

Deutsch

German

German-speaking countries

	Austria
	Germany
	Liechtenstein
	Luxembourg
	Switzerland

A short history of German

German was originally the language spoken by tribes in the area of central Europe that was not conquered by the Romans. This explains why it has developed in a different way from the Romance languages like Italian and Spanish.

The first example of the written language comes from the 8th century, but it was Martin Luther's version of the Bible, published in 1534, which spread the language most widely. Today, German is spoken officially in a group of neighboring countries: Germany, Austria, Switzerland, Luxembourg and Liechtenstein.

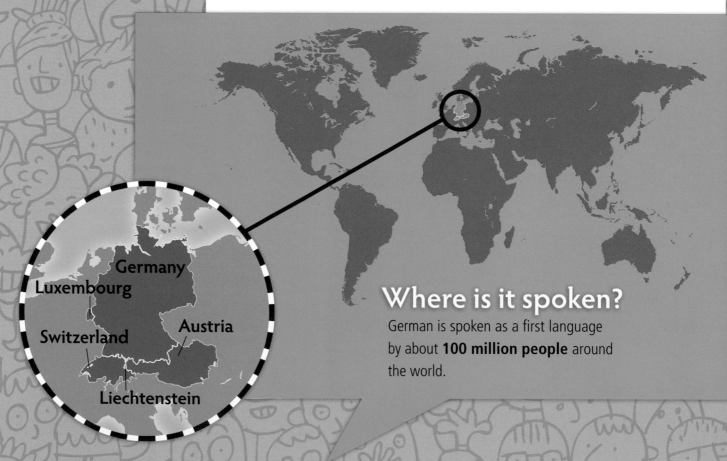

Germany
Luxembourg
Switzerland
Austria
Liechtenstein

Where is it spoken?

German is spoken as a first language by about **100 million people** around the world.

Greetings

Guten Tag	Hello
Auf Wiedersehen/ Tschüs!	Goodbye/Bye
Mein name ist...	My name is. . .
Wie geht's?	How are you?
Es geht mir gut, danke	I'm fine, thank you
Es geht mir nicht so gut	Not so good

Numbers

1	eins	6	sechs
2	zwei	7	sieben
3	drei	8	acht
4	vier	9	neun
5	fünf	10	zehn

Pronunciation points

ei   in **drei** is pronounced like "i" in "hide"

ie   in **vier** sounds like "ee" in "beer"

When you see two dots, called an "umlaut," written above a vowel, it means that the sound changes.

u   is usually an "oo" sound, but the **ü** in **tschüs** is like the "ew" in "few" with your lips pressed together

o   is usually like the "o" in "low," but the **ö** sounds more like the "i" in "girl"

ch   as in **acht**, is not found in English. It's an "h" sound in the middle of your mouth.

s   at the beginning of a word is like "z" in "zoo." An example is **sechs**.

Speak German!

Guten Tag. Wie geht's?	Hello, how are you?
Es geht mir gut, danke	I'm fine, thanks
Mein name ist Sabine. Wie heisst du?	My name is Sabine. What are you called?
Mein name ist Katie. Bis morgen	I'm Katie. See you later
Prima! Tschüs	Great! Goodbye

Language matters

Some very long German words are made by putting several nouns together to make one word. **Höchstgeschwind-igkeitsbegrenzung** means "maximum speed limit."

German is the only world language which begins all nouns with a capital letter. The place name **Berlin** and the word **Baum**, meaning "tree," both start with a capital "B."

Aa *a* umlaut
Ää *a* umlaut
Bb *be*
Cc *tse*
Dd *de*
Ee *e*
Ff *ef*
Gg *ge*
Hh *haa*
Ii *i*
Jj *yot*
Kk *ka*
Ll *el*
Mm *em*
Nn *en*
Oo *o*
Öö *o* umlaut
Pp *pe*
Qq *ku*
Rr *er*
Ss *es*
Tt *te*
Uu *u*
Üü *u* umlaut
Vv *fau*
Ww *ve*
Xx *ix*
Yy *üpsilon*
Zz *tset*
ß *scharfes s*

Dansk

Danish

Danish-speaking countries

 Denmark

 Faroe Islands

 Greenland

A short history of Danish

Danish developed from the Old Norse language. It was originally written in an ancient alphabet called Runic. This was replaced in the Middle Ages by the Latin alphabet.

For 400 years, Denmark ruled over Norway. Danish was the official language of Norway until 1814. The two countries share an almost identical writing system and have a good understanding of each other's language. Swedish is also similar to Danish, but it doesn't have as much in common with it as Norwegian. Danish was the official language of Iceland until 1944 and is still learned there. It was also an official language of Greenland until 2009.

Greenland

Faroe Islands

Denmark

Where is it spoken?

Danish is spoken by over **5 million people** around the world.

Greetings

Hej	Hello
Hej hej	Goodbye
Mit navn er...	My name is. . .
Hvordan går det?	How are you?
Godt tak	I'm fine, thank you
Jeg er syg	I'm not well

Numbers

1	en	6	seks
2	to	7	syv
3	tre	8	otte
4	fire	9	ni
5	fem	10	ti

Pronunciation points

y   in the word **syv** is pronounced like "ew" in "few"

r   is a very guttural sound, vibrated at the back of your throat

ej   in **hej** sounds very similar to the English "i" in "hi"

Danish has two more vowels than English, and these have accent marks:

å   in the word **går** sounds like "o" in "old"

ø   in **Jørgen** sounds like "ei" in "weird"

When "g" follows another consonant, as in "morgen," it is not pronounced at all.

Speak Danish!

Hej. Hvordan går det? — Hello, how are you?

Godt tak — I'm fine, thanks

Mit navn er Jørgen. Hvar hedder du? — My name is Jørgen. What are you called?

Mit navn er Jim. Vi ses i morgen — I'm Jim. See you tomorrow

Fantastisk! Hej hej — Great! Goodbye

Language matters

Danish has long words that are made of several, shorter, joined-up nouns. For example, **Kvindehåndboldlandsholdet** means "the female handball national team."

Danish nouns are divided into two types: common or neuter. The word for "a" is **en** with common nouns and **et** with neuter nouns. "A boy, a girl" are **en dreng**, **en pige**, but "a house" is **et hus**, as the word **hus** is neuter.

To say "the boy," "the girl" or "the house," you put **en** or **et** on the end of the noun: **drengen**, **pigen**, **huset**.

Aa Bb Cc Dd Ee Ff Gg Hh Ii Jj Kk Ll Mm Nn Oo Pp Qq Rr Ss Tt Uu Vv Ww Xx Yy Zz Æø Øø Åå

a be se de ae aef ge hå i yåd kå ael aem aen o pe ku aer aes te oo ve dobbelt-ve aeks y saet æ ø å

Nederlands

Dutch

Dutch-speaking countries

 Belgium
 Dutch Antilles

Netherlands

Suriname

A short history of Dutch

Modern Dutch began to emerge around the 15th century. As with the other Germanic languages, a key moment was the publication of the first translation of the Bible. This happened in 1619 and helped to spread the written language.

During the period of the Dutch Empire, from the 17th century, the language moved east to Indonesia. It also spread west to Suriname and the Dutch Antilles, where it is still an official language. At the same time, Afrikaans (South Africa's third language) developed from the dialects of Dutch settlers.

Dutch is spoken not just in the Netherlands but also in the northern part of Belgium, where it is called Flemish.

Netherlands

Belgium

Dutch Antilles

Suriname

Where is it spoken?

Dutch is spoken as a first language by over **22 million people** around the world.

28

Greetings

Hallo	Hello
Tot ziens	Goodbye
Ik heet...	My name is. . .
Hoe gaat het?	How are you?
Goed, dank je	I'm fine, thank you
Ik voel me niet goed	I'm not so good

Numbers

1	een	6	zes
2	twee	7	zeven
3	drie	8	acht
4	vier	9	negen
5	vijf	10	tien

Pronunciation points

The Dutch alphabet is exactly the same as the English alphabet, although vowels are pronounced differently, particularly when there are two vowels together.

ee in the word **een** is like the "ay" in "bay"

eu in **neus** (nose) sounds like "oh" with your lips pressed together

oe in the word **goed** is like the "oo" in "book"

ij in the word **vijf** is like the "i" in "mine"

g in the word **goed** is like a strongly pronounced "h"

ch in the word **acht** is an "h" sound pronounced at the back of your throat

Speak Dutch!

Hallo. Hoe gaat het? — Hello, how are you?

Goed, dank je — I'm fine, thanks

Ik heet Kim. Hoe heet je? — My name is Kim. What are you called?

Ik heet Kieron. Tot morgen — I'm Kieron. See you tomorrow

Geweldig! Tot ziens — Great! Goodbye

Language matters

Many Dutch words are similar to English ones, such as names for everyday things like fruit: **appel**, **peer**, **banana**.

Dutch makes use of little words such as **maar** and **hoor** to change the mood of a sentence. They can make a command sound more polite or a request more urgent. **Kom maar hoor** is a friendly "Come along now" instead of the more curt **Kom.**

Dutch has two words for "the." With masculine and feminine nouns it uses **de**. For neuter nouns it uses **het**.

Aa	a
Bb	be
Cc	se
Dd	de
Ee	e
Ff	ef
Gg	he
Hh	ha
Ii	i
Jj	je
Kk	ke
Ll	el
Mm	em
Nn	en
Oo	o
Pp	pe
Qq	ku
Rr	er
Ss	es
Tt	te
Uu	u
Vv	fe
Ww	ve
Xx	ix
Yy	ei
Zz	zet

Spanish

Spanish-speaking countries

Can you find them on the map?

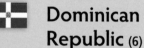

Argentina (17)

Bolivia (15)

Chile (16)

Colombia (12)

Costa Rica (8)

Cuba (5)

Dominican Republic (6)

Ecuador (13)

El Salvador (3)

Equatorial Guinea (21)

Guatemala (2)

Honduras (4)

Mexico (1)

Nicaragua (9)

Panama (10)

Paraguay (19)

Peru (14)

Puerto Rico (7)

Spain (20)

Uruguay (18)

Venezuela (11)

A short history of Spanish

Spanish began as a version of Latin. It grew up in the Iberian Peninsula during the Roman occupation (210 BC–AD 476).

The country was invaded in 711 by Arabic-speaking Moors. They brought new things and new words for them, like **albaricoque** (apricot). The Spanish that we know today spread from the north of the country when the territory occupied by the Moors was reconquered by the Christians.

Between the 15th and 17th centuries, Spain became a world power and colonized much of South America. That is why Spanish is spoken in countries from Mexico to Argentina. Recently it has become the second language of the USA.

Where is it spoken?
Spanish is spoken by around
420 million people.

30

Greetings

Hola	Hello
Adiós	Goodbye
Me llamo...	My name is…
¿Cómo estás?	How are you?
Muy bien, gracias	I'm fine, thank you
No me siento bien	I don't feel so good

Numbers

1	uno	6	seis
2	dos	7	siete
3	tres	8	ocho
4	cuatro	9	nueve
5	cinco	10	diez

Pronunciation points

Spanish letters are always pronounced the same way. Accents are used to show where a word is emphasized, as in **adiós** or in question words like **¿qué?** and **¿cómo?**

h	is never pronounced, so **hola** sounds like "ola"
z, ci and **ce**	in European Spanish, words like **diez**, **cinco** and **cero** all sound like "th" in "thumb"
ll	in **llamo** is like the "y" in "yes"
ñ	in **mañana** is like the "ni" sound in "onion"
qu	is like "c" in "cat"

rr or **r** at the beginning of a word, like **Rafa**, is a sound made by vibrating the tip of your tongue against the top of your mouth.

Speak Spanish!

Hola. ¿Qué tal?	Hello, how are you?
Muy bien, gracias	I'm fine, thanks
Me llamo Rafa. ¿Tú, cómo te llamas?	My name is Rafa. What are you called?
Me llamo Martha. Nos vemos mañana	I'm Martha. See you tomorrow
¡Estupendo! Adiós	Great! Goodbye

Language matters

All nouns are either masculine or feminine. There are also different words for "the." **El** goes in front of masculine nouns, **la** in front of feminine nouns. So **la limonada** means "the lemonade" and **el café** means "the coffee."

In written Spanish, questions have an upside-down question mark at the beginning as well as an upright one at the end: **¿Cómo te llamas?** (What's your name?) The same goes for exclamation marks: **¡Cuidado!** (Be careful!)

Verbs have different endings, which tell you who or what the subject is. **Vivo** means "I live," **vivimos** means "we live."

Spanish is called **Español** or **Castellano**, which means "Castilian." This refers to the region of Castile where it was first spoken. This distinguishes it from other languages spoken in Spain, such as Catalan around Barcelona.

Aa *a* · Bb *be* · Cc *ce* · Dd *de* · Ee *e* · Ff *efe* · Gg *ge* · Hh *hache* · Ii *i* · Jj *jota* · Kk *ka* · Ll *ele* · Mm *eme* · Nn *ene* · Ññ *eñe* · Oo *o* · Pp *pe* · Qq *cu* · Rr *erre* · Ss *ese* · Tt *te* · Uu *u* · Vv *uve* · Ww *uve doble* · Xx *equis* · Yy *i griega* · Zz *zeta*

Português

Portuguese

Portuguese-speaking countries

 Angola

Brazil

Cape Verde

Guinea-Bissau

Mozambique

Portugal

São Tomé and Príncipe

A short history of Portuguese

Portuguese developed from the Latin that was spoken in the north-western corner of modern-day Spain during the Roman occupation. When Portugal became an independent country in 1143, Portuguese became its national language. Portugal's extensive discoveries and conquests during the 15th and 16th centuries led to it becoming a widely spoken language.

In South America, Brazilian Portuguese is spoken by 190 million people. It has developed a different accent and some different vocabulary from the language of Portugal. Portuguese is also spoken in the African countries that used to be Portuguese colonies: Angola, Mozambique, Guinea-Bissau and Cape Verde.

Portugal

Cape Verde

Guinea-Bissau

Angola

Brazil

São Tomé & Príncipe

Mozambique

Where is it spoken?

Portuguese is spoken by well over **200 million people** around the world as a first language.

Greetings

Olá	Hello
Adeus	Goodbye
Meu nome é…	My name is…
Como vai?	How are you?
Bem, obrigado/obrigada	I'm fine, thank you (male/female)
Não estou bem	I'm not so well

Numbers

1	um	6	seis
2	dois	7	sete
3	três	8	oito
4	quatro	9	nove
5	cinco	10	dez

Pronunciation points

Accents are used to show where you emphasize a word and when a vowel has a different sound.

ã and **õ** are nasal sounds. They are spoken down your nose.

em in **bem** is another nasal sound. It is pronounced like "ang" in "bang."

ç in a word like **almoço** (lunch) sounds like the "s" in "sad"

nh in a word like **amanhã** (tomorrow) sounds like "ni" in "onion"

ch in **chama** sounds like "sh" in "cash"

In Brazilian Portuguese the **r**, as in **Rio de Janeiro**, can sound more like a strongly pronounced English "h"

h is not pronounced at all

Speak Portuguese!

Olá. Como vai? — Hello, how are you?

Bem, obrigado — I'm fine, thanks

Meu nome é Luisa. Come te chamas? — My name is Luisa. What are you called?

Meu nome é Harry. Até amanhã — My name's Harry. See you tomorrow

Ótimo! Adeus — Great! Goodbye

Language matters

A or **o** is used in front of people's names when you're talking about them. **A** for female and **o** for male: **a Maria**, **o Ronaldo**.

Portuguese people are fond of adding **–inho** or **–inha** to words. It's a friendly, chatty equivalent of "little": **caffezinho** (small coffee), **Ronaldinho** (little Ronaldo).

The Portuguese alphabet has 26 letters. The letters **K**, **W** and **Y**, though, are only used in foreign words.

Aa bê · Bb bê · Cc cê · Dd dê · Ee é · Ff efe · Gg gê · Hh agá · Ii i · Jj jota · Kk cá · Ll ele · Mm eme · Nn ene · Oo ó · Pp pê · Qq quê · Rr erre · Ss esse · Tt tê · Uu u · Vv vê · Ww dábliu · Xx xis · Yy ípsilon · Zz zê

French

French-speaking countries

Can you find them on the map?

- 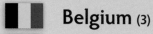 **Belgium** (3)
- **Benin** (14)
- **Burkina Faso** (11)
- **Canada** (1)
- **Central African Republic** (15)
- **Democratic Republic of Congo** (17)
- **France** (2)
- **Gabon** (16)
- **Guinea** (10)
- **Haiti** (20)
- **Ivory Coast** (12)
- **Luxembourg** (4)
- **Madagascar** (19)
- **Mali** (8)
- **Monaco** (6)
- **Niger** (9)
- **Senegal** (7)
- **Seychelles** (18)
- **Switzerland** (5)
- **Togo** (13)

A short history of French

French is one of the European Romance languages that had its origins in Latin. It also inherited words that came from the Celtic people who lived there before the Roman conquest in 50 BC.

For many years there were different languages spoken in the south of the country and in the north. After the French Revolution in 1789, the language of Paris became the country's official language.

France was an important colonial power and used to have control over many other countries. As a result, French is still spoken in countries in Africa and the Caribbean, as well as Quebec, in Canada. There are also overseas "departments" which are governed by France, including Guadeloupe, Martinique and French Guiana.

Where is it spoken?

French is spoken by **115 million people** around the world.

Greetings

Bonjour	Hello
Au revoir	Goodbye
Je m'appelle…	My name is…
Ça va?	How are you?
Ça va bien, merci	I'm fine, thank you
Pas si bien	Not so good

Numbers

1	un	6	six
2	deux	7	sept
3	trois	8	huit
4	quatre	9	neuf
5	cinq	10	dix

Pronunciation points

s is like an English "s" at the beginning of a word, like **sept**. In the middle of a word, like **maison** (house), it sounds like a "z." When it appears at the end of a word, like **trois**, it is not pronounced at all.

ç in a word like **ça** sounds like "s" in "sum"

j in **je**, **ge** in **génial** and **gi** in **girafe** sound like the "s" in "vision"

th in word like **thé** sounds like "t"

é in **génial** sounds like "ay" in "say," and **è** is like the "e" in "bed." **E** at the end of **quatre** is not pronounced.

u in **tu** is pronounced as a German **ü**, like "ee" said with pursed lips. **Un**, as in **un**, is a nasal sound like "euh."

qu in **quatre** sounds like "k"

h is not pronounced at all (**hôtel**)

Speak French!

Bonjour. Ça va?
Hello, how are you?

Ça va bien, merci
I'm fine, thanks

Je m'appelle Marine. Tu t'appelles comment?
My name is Marine. What are you called?

Je m'appelle Kelly. À demain!
My name's Kelly. See you tomorrow

Génial! Au revoir
Great! Goodbye

Language matters

French has two words for "you": **vous** and **tu**. When children speak to an adult they say **vous**, except with their parents, when they use the word **tu**. **Tu** is always used among friends.

French verbs have different endings, depending on the subject: **je parle** (I speak), **tu parles** (you speak), **nous parlons** (we speak).

If you want to say that something belongs to someone, you need to use the word **de**. "Pierre's friend" in French would be **l'ami de Pierre**, literally "the friend of Pierre."

Aa a Bb bé Cc cé Dd dé Ee e Ff eff Gg gé Hh ache Ii i Jj gi Kk ka Ll ell Mm emme Nn enne Oo o Pp pé Qq qu Rr erre Ss esse Tt té Uu u Vv vé Ww double-vé Xx ixe Yy i grec Zz zède

Italiano

Italian

Italian-speaking countries

 Italy

 San Marino

 Switzerland

 Vatican City

A short history of Italian

Italian is the Romance language with the closest connections to Latin, as they both originated in the country we now call Italy. When Italy became a unified nation in 1861, there were a number of different regional dialects and languages spoken across the country. The one chosen to be the official language came from the region of Tuscany, around Florence. Nowadays Italian is one of the four official languages of Switzerland, as well as being spoken in the Vatican City and San Marino. There are also large Italian-speaking immigrant communities in the USA and Australia.

Italian has provided the world with many words connected with food, such as spaghetti and pizza, and music, such as piano.

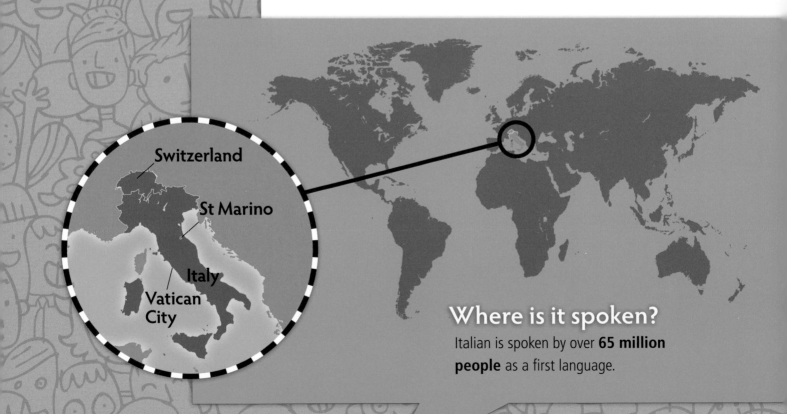

Switzerland
St Marino
Italy
Vatican City

Where is it spoken?
Italian is spoken by over **65 million people** as a first language.

Greetings

Buongiorno	Hello
Arrivederci/ciao	Goodbye/Bye
Mi chiamo…	My name is…
Come stai?	How are you?
Sto bene grazie	I'm fine, thank you
Non mi sento bene	I don't feel well

Numbers

1	uno	6	sei
2	due	7	sette
3	tre	8	otto
4	quattro	9	nove
5	cinque	10	dieci

Pronunciation points

Italian is famous for the sing-song way in which it is spoken (its intonation).

The **c** before **i** in **ciao** (or before **e**) sounds like "ch" in "chin"

g before **i** in **buongiorno** (or before **e**) sounds like "g" in "gentle"

ch in **chiamo** is like "c" in "case"

gli is like "ll" in "million," and **gn** is like the "ny" in "canyon"

h in a word like **ho** (I have) is silent

z at the beginning of a word, like **zero**, sounds like "dz" and in a word like **grazie** it sounds like "ts"

In double consonants like **zz**, both are pronounced quite clearly, as in **pizza**.

Accents are only used at the end of words: **città** (city).

Speak Italian!

Buongiorno. Come stai? — Hello, how are you?

Sto bene grazie — I'm fine, thanks

Mi chiamo Gianni. E tu, come ti chiami? — My name is Gianni. What are you called?

Mi chiamo Lee. Ci vediamo domani — I'm Lee. See you tomorrow

Fantastico! Ciao — Great! Goodbye

Language matters

Italian has three words for "a." As well as **un** before masculine words and **una** before feminine words, there's also **uno**. It goes in front of some words beginning with **s** and **z**, like **uno sdraio** (a deck chair). The same thing occurs with the word for "the," which can be **il**, **la** or **lo**: **lo sdraio** (the deck chair).

To make nouns plural you change the ending. Nouns like **ragazza** (girl) change the **a** to an **e**: **due ragazze** (two girls). Nouns that end in **o** usually change their ending to **i**, so **un gatto** (one cat) becomes **due gatti** (two cats).

Aa *a* · Bb *bi* · Cc *ci* · Dd *di* · Ee *e* · Ff *effe* · Gg *gi* · Hh *acca* · Ii *i* · Jj *i-lunga* · Kk *kappa* · Ll *elle* · Mm *emme* · Nn *enne* · Oo *o* · Pp *pi* · Qq *cu* · Rr *erre* · Ss *esse* · Tt *ti* · Uu *u* · Vv *vu* · Ww *vu doppia* · Xx *ics* · Yy *i greca* · Zz *zeta*

Русский
(Russkiy)

Russian

Russian-speaking countries

 Belarus

 Kazakhstan

 Kyrgyzstan

 Russia

 Ukraine

A short history of Russian

Russian has its origins in the area around Kiev, which is now the capital of Ukraine. It spread partly through the teachings of the Orthodox Church.

Modern Russian, based on the language spoken in Moscow, was first given a written form in the 18th century.

In the 20th century, a number of states became independent from the rule of Russia. These included Ukraine, Belarus, Kazakhstan and Kyrgyzstan. Although these countries have their own languages, they still have large numbers of Russian speakers. This helps to make Russian the most widely spoken native language in Europe.

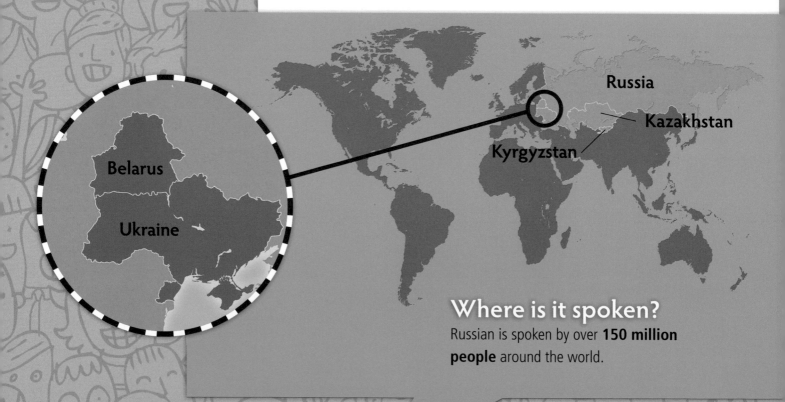

Where is it spoken?
Russian is spoken by over **150 million people** around the world.

38

Greetings

Zdravstvujtye	Hello
Da svidaniya	Goodbye
Myenya zavoot…	My name is…
Kak dyela?	How are you?
Syoh khorosho, spaseeba	I'm fine, thank you
Nye ochyen khorosho	I'm not very well

Numbers

1	adeen	6	shest
2	dva	7	syem
3	tree	8	vosyem
4	chyetirye	9	dyevyat
5	pyat	10	dyesyat

Pronunciation points

You pronounce both **d** and **v** in a word like **dva**.

kh in **khorosho** is a strong guttural "h" sound

r in a word like **zavtra** is rolled

Russian vowels have different sounds when they are emphasized.

Ye sounds like "yay" in the middle of **chyetirye**. This is the stressed syllable. But at the end of the word the **ye** sounds like "ee." That's because it is an unstressed syllable.

You write **khorosho** but it sounds like **huh-rah-shoh**. This is because the last syllable **shoh** is the stressed one, so that's where the **o** sounds strongly.

Lots of Russian words have three or four consonants in a row. The best way to pronounce them is to break them up into bits (syllables). **Zdravstvujtye** sounds like **zdrah-stvooy-tee**.

Speak Russian!

Zdravstvujtye, kak dyela?	Hello, how are you?
Syoh khorosho, spaseeba	I'm fine, thanks
Myenya zavoot Daria. Kak vas zavoot?	My name is Daria. What are you called?
Myenya zavoot Lisa. Da zavtra	I'm Lisa. See you tomorrow
Otlichno! Da svidaniya	Great! Goodbye

Language matters

There are two ways of addressing someone as "you." The friendly **ty** and the polite **vy**.

The Russian alphabet is called Cyrillic. It has 33 characters. Six of them look and sound the same as those of the Latin alphabet: **A**, **E**, **K**, **M**, **O** and **T**.

Cyrillic	Sound
Аа	a
Бб	b
Вв	v
Гг	g
Дд	d
Ее	ye
Ёё	yo
Жж	zh
Зз	z
Ии	i
Йй	y
Кк	k
Лл	l
Мм	m
Нн	n
Оо	o
Пп	p
Рр	r
Сс	s
Тт	t
Уу	oo
Фф	f
Хх	kh
Цц	ts
Чч	ch
Шш	sh
Щщ	shch
ъ	pause
Ыы	ei
Ьь	softy
Ээ	e
Юю	yu
Яя	ya

Polszczyzna

Polish

Polish-speaking countries

Poland

A short history of Polish

Polish is based on a language spoken by people who lived in the area between the Vistula and Odra rivers. Around the 10th century, this area was united into the first Polish state. In the 15th century, Christian missionaries introduced the Latin alphabet, which made it possible to write Polish. Until then Polish had only been a spoken language. The first Polish dictionary was published in 1807.

In 1989, when Russian-backed communist rule was overthrown, Polish became the country's official language. There are also big Polish-speaking communities in Argentina, Australia, Belarus, Brazil, Canada, Germany, Lithuania, the UK, Ukraine, the USA and Russia.

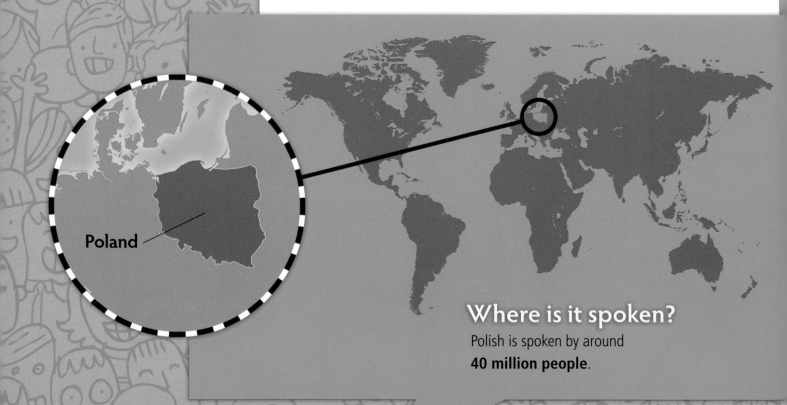

Poland

Where is it spoken?

Polish is spoken by around **40 million people**.

Greetings

Cześć	Hello
Do widzenia	Goodbye
Mam na imię...	My name is…
Co słychać?	How are you?
Dobrze, dziękuję	I'm fine, thank you
Źle się czuję	I'm not well

Numbers

1	jeden	6	sześć
2	dwa	7	siedem
3	trzy	8	osiem
4	cztery	9	dziewięć
5	pięć	10	dziesięć

Pronunciation points

ę	in **się** is a nasal sound like "eh"
ć	in **pieć** sounds like "ch" in "chin"
ś	in **sześć** sounds like "sh" in "sugar"
ł	in **słychać** sounds like "w" in "wit"
c	in **co** sounds like "ts" in "cuts"
sz	in **sześć** sounds like "sh" in "ship"
cz	in **cześć** sounds like "ch" in "cherry"

Speak Polish!

Cześć. Co słychać? — Hello, how are you?

Dobrze, dziękuję — I'm fine, thanks

Mam na imię Paweł. Jak się pan nazywasz? — My name is Pavel. What are you called?

Mam na imię Adam. Do zobaczenia jutro — My name is Adam. See you tomorrow

Świetnie! Do widzenia — Great! Goodbye

Language matters

Polish does not have words for "a," "an" and "the." The word **dom** can mean either "a house" or "the house."

Polish nouns have three genders: masculine, feminine and neuter. Masculine nouns usually end in a consonant, for example: **nos** (nose). Feminine nouns generally end in **-a**, for example **lampa** (lamp). Neuter nouns end in **-o** as in **dziecko** (child).

Verb endings change depending on who is doing the action. **Czytać** means "to read"; **czytam** is "I read"; **czyta** is "he" or "she reads"; **czytamy** is "we read."

Q, V and **X** are not part of the Polish alphabet. They are only used in foreign words.

Aa *a* Ąą *ą* Bb *be* Cc *ce* Ćć *cie* Dd *de* Ee *e* Ęę *ę* Ff *ef* Gg *gie* Hh *ha* Ii *i* Jj *jot* Kk *ka* Ll *el* Łł *eł* Mm *em* Nn *en* Oo *o* Óó *o z kreską* Pp *pe* Rr *er* Ss *es* Śś *eś* Tt *te* Uu *u* Ww *wu* Yy *igrek* Zz *zet* Źź *ziet* Żż *żet*

हिन्दी-उर्दू
(Hindi)

Hindi-Urdu

Hindi-Urdu–speaking countries

 India

 Pakistan

A short history of Hindi-Urdu

The two languages Hindi and Urdu are spoken in the north and west of the Indian subcontinent. When spoken, they sound virtually identical and have very similar grammar, which is why they are treated as one language. But they have completely different scripts and lots of different vocabulary, although they both have their roots in the ancient language of Sanskrit.

After nearly 100 years of British rule, the Indian subcontinent was divided, in 1947, into the independent countries of Pakistan and India. Urdu became the official language of Pakistan and Hindi the official language of India.

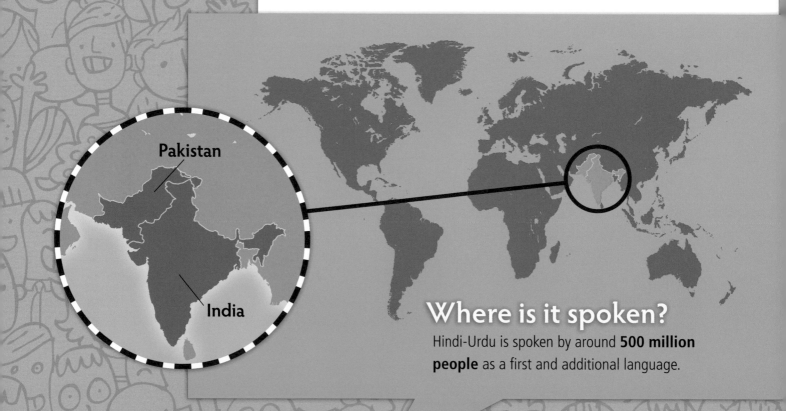

Pakistan

India

Where is it spoken?

Hindi-Urdu is spoken by around **500 million people** as a first and additional language.

Hindi greetings

Namaste	Hello/Goodbye
Mera naam … hain	My name is…
Tum kaise ho?	How are you?
Main theek hoon, dhanyavad	I'm fine, thank you
Main theek nahin hoon	I'm not so well

Numbers

1	ek	6	che
2	doh	7	saat
3	teen	8	aat
4	char	9	nau
5	panch	10	das

Pronunciation points

These sounds are based on the Hindi alphabet of 11 vowels and 35 consonants.

a   in **namaste** sounds like the "u" in "hut"

aa   in **aapka** sounds like the "a" in "father"

e   in **mera** is like the "ai" sound in "maid"

o   in **doh** sounds like the "oa" in "moan"

th   in **theek** is a breathy sounding "th" as in "thin"

dh   in **dhanyavad** is a breathy "h" sound added to the "d"

in   in **hain** is a nasal sound like "ng" in "bang"

Speak Hindi!

Namaste. Tum kaise ho? — Hello, how are you?

Main theek hoon, dhanyavad — I'm fine, thanks

Mera naam Shanta hain. Aapka naam kya hain? — My name is Shanta. What are you called?

Mera naam Gary hain. Kal milenge — My name is Gary. See you tomorrow

Accha! Namaste — Great! Goodbye

Language matters

Hindi doesn't have articles, words for "the," "an" or "a."

Verbs always go to the end of sentences. For example, the question "How are you?" is **Tum kaise ho?** A word-for-word translation is "You how are?"

The alphabet shown here is written in the Hindi Devanagari script, which you read from left to right. A distinctive line at the top of letters links them together. Urdu, on the other hand, is based on Arabic and is written and read from right to left.

The English version of the Devanagari alphabet uses extra symbols. A dot below a letter means that it is pronounced with your tongue touching the roof of your mouth.

अ आ इ ई उ ऊ ऋ ए ऐ ओ औ अं अः क ख ग घ ङ च छ ज झ ञ ट ठ ड ढ ण त थ द ध न प फ ब भ म य र ल व श ष स ह

a aa i ee u uu r e ai o au am ah ka kha ga gha ṅa ca cha ja jha ña ṭa ṭha ḍa ḍha ṇa ta tha da dha na pa pha ba bha ma ya ra la va śa ṣa sa ha

Bengali

বাংলা
(Bangla)

Bengali-speaking countries

 Bangladesh
State of West Bengal (India)

A short history of Bengali

Bengali grew up around 1,000 years ago in the area of Bengal, in the north-eastern region of the Indian subcontinent. Similar to other Indo-European languages from this area, it has a writing system that came originally from Sanskrit. The first dictionary and grammar books were written by a Portuguese missionary in the 18th century.

Bengali was granted official language status in Bangladesh in 1954. The first non-European writer to win the Nobel Prize for literature was a Bengali writer, Rabindranath Tagore (in 1913). He did a great deal to modernize the language.

Bengali has words from Arabic and Hindi, which explains the different ways of saying hello.

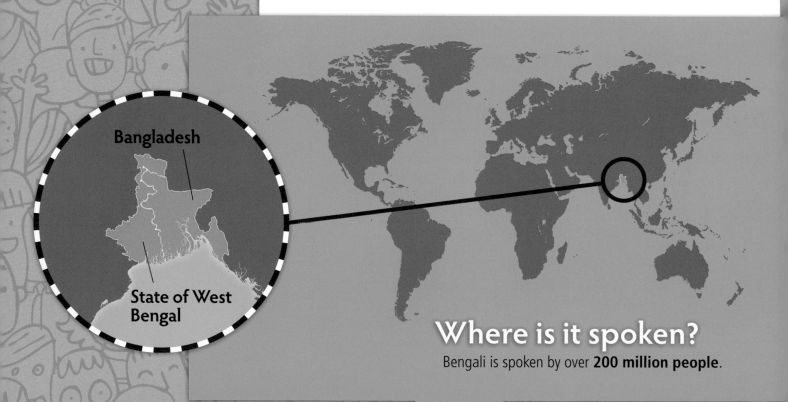

Bangladesh

State of West Bengal

Where is it spoken?
Bengali is spoken by over **200 million people**.

Greetings

Nomaashkaar	Hello (among Hindus)
Asalaam alaykum	Hello (among Muslims)
Aabar dakha hobe	Goodbye (See you again)
Amar nam...	My name is…
Tumi kamon aacho?	How are you?
Aami bhaalo aachi	I'm fine, thank you
Aami bhaalo noi	I'm not well

Numbers

1	ek	6	ch-hoy
2	dui	7	shaat
3	tin	8	aat
4	chaar	9	noy
5	paach	10	dosh

Pronunciation points

aa in **chaar** sounds like the "a" in "father"

i in **tin** sounds like a shortened "ee" in "seen"

u in **tumi** sounds like "oo" in "hood"

uu sounds like "oo" in "roof"

e in **ek** is pronounced as "ay" in "pay." In some words, it's pronounced as "e" in "echo" or "a" in "apple."

bh in **bhaalo** is pronounced as "b-h" in "tub-hot," with the two sounds running together

ch-h in **ch-hoy** is pronounced as "ch-h" in "staunch-heart," again with the two sounds running together

Speak Bengali!

Nomaashkaar. Tumi kamon aacho? — Hello, how are you?

Aami bhaalo aachi — I'm fine, thanks

Amar nam Suresh. Tomar nam ki? — My name is Suresh. What are you called?

Amar nam Julia. Kaal dakhaa hobe — I'm Julia. See you tomorrow

Ṭhik achhe! Aabar dakha hobe — Great! See you again

Language matters

Bengali is written from left to right. The Bengali script is similar to the Devanagari alphabet used in Hindi. There are no capital letters. All the letters have a bar or a partial bar at the top, which connects to the other letters in a word.

Vowels are assumed to be there even if they are not written down, as with the Arabic script (see page 13). Letters with a dot below them are pronounced with your tongue touching the roof of your mouth.

Kiswahili

Swahili

Swahili-speaking countries

 Comoros Islands

 Democratic Republic of Congo

 Kenya

 Swaziland

 Tanzania

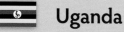 Uganda

A short history of Swahili

Swahili-speaking people live on the eastern shores of Africa, beside the Indian Ocean. It is thought that the language has been spoken in this territory for more than 1,000 years. The earliest known documents written in Swahili date from 1711.

When Germany, and then Britain, colonized this region in the 19th century, there were many local languages spoken. Swahili was chosen as the official language. Among the many dialects of Swahili, the dialect of Zanzibar was selected as the basis for the standard written language. Swahili, called Kiswahili by its speakers, is now mainly spoken as a second or additional language. Well-known words are **safari** (journey) and **simba** (lion).

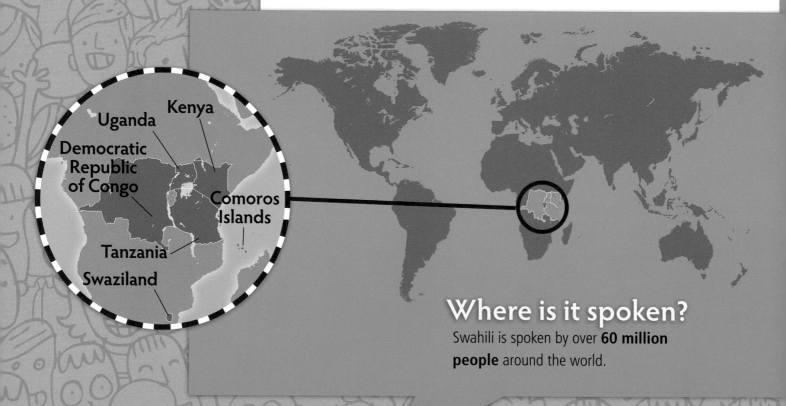

Where is it spoken?

Swahili is spoken by over **60 million people** around the world.

Greetings

Jambo	Hello
Kwaheri	Goodbye
Jina langu ni...	My name is…
Habari gani?	How are you?
Sijambo, asante	I'm fine, thank you
Sijisikii vizuri	Not so good

Numbers

1	moja		6	sita
2	mbili		7	saba
3	tatu		8	nane
4	nne		9	tisa
5	tano		10	kumi

Pronunciation points

a	sounds like "a" in "father"
e	sounds like "e" in "get"
i	sounds like "ee" in "feet"
o	sounds like "oo" in "door"
u	sounds like "oo" in "moon"
j	in **sijambo** is pronounced like "j" in "jam"
th	sounds like "th" in "thank"
dh	sounds like "th" in "there"
ng	sounds like "ng" in "jingles"
ng'	sounds like "ng" in "sing"
m	plus another consonant, as in **mbili**, sounds like "m" with a closed mouth
n	plus another consonant, as in **nzuri**, sounds like "n" with your mouth half-closed

Speak Swahili!

Jambo. Habari gani?	Hello, how are you?
Sijambo, asante	I'm fine, thank you
Jina langu ni Kesha. Jina lako nani?	My name is Kesha. What are you called?
Jina langu ni Zoe. Tutaonana kesho	I'm Zoe. See you tomorrow
Nzuri! Kwaheri	Great! Goodbye

Language matters

Nouns are divided into types, or classes, based on the kind of noun they are and the way that they are spelled. For example, the class of nouns beginning with **m-** in the singular and **wa-** in the plural is used for people and animals. **Mtu** means "person" and **watu** means "people."

You change the tense of the verb by adding short words to the front of it. These are called prefixes. You use **-na-** to show the present and **-ta-** to show the future. **A** stands for "he" or "she." **Enda** means "to go," so **anaenda** is "he/she goes," **ataenda**, "she/he will go."

Aa a
Bb be
CHch che
Dd de
Ee e
Ff ef
Gg ge
Hh he
Ii i
Jj je
Kk ke
Ll le
Mm me
Nn ne
Oo o
Pp pe
Rr re
Ss se
Tt te
Uu u
Vv ve
Ww we
Yy ye
Zz ze

Zulu

Isizulu

Zulu-speaking countries

 South Africa

Zimbabwe

A short history of Zulu

The Zulu people are thought to have settled in South Africa around 1,000 years ago.

Zulu did not have a written form until missionaries from Europe arrived. They wrote down the language using the Latin script. The first grammar book of the Zulu language was published in Norway in 1850 by a Norwegian missionary.

The language has several click sounds. These are sounds made in your mouth without using your voice box.

The language is mostly spoken in the South African region of KwaZulu Natal, which means "Land of-the Zulu." It is also spoken in Zimbabwe, where it is called Ndebele.

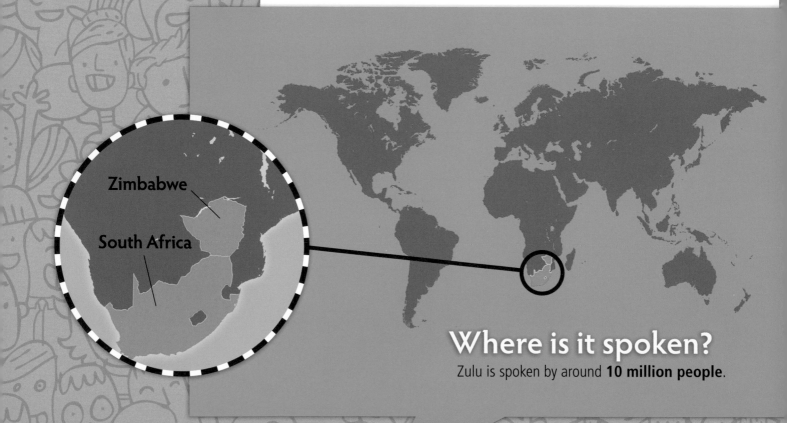

Zimbabwe

South Africa

Where is it spoken?
Zulu is spoken by around **10 million people**.

Greetings

Sawubona	Hello (to one person)
Sanibonani	Hello (to several people)
Hamba kahle/ Sala kahle	Goodbye (to person leaving/to person staying)
Igama lami ngu...	My name is…
Unjani?	How are you?
Ngikhona ngiyabonga	I'm okay, thanks
Angizizwa kahle	I don't feel well

Numbers

1	kunye	6	yisithupa
2	kubili	7	yisikhombisa
3	kuthathu	8	yisishiyagalombili
4	kune	9	yisishiyagalolunye
5	kuhlanu	10	yishum

Pronunciation points

Zulu uses click noises made in your mouth.

c   in a word like **cha** (no) sounds like sucking teeth in irritation

q   in a word like **iqanda** (zero) is like a bottle cork popping

x   in **uxolo** (excuse me) sounds like the clicking noise people make to encourage a horse

tsh   sounds like "ch" in "cheese"

ng   in **ngisaphila** sounds like "ng" in "linger"

Zulu is also a tonal language. The meaning of some words depends on how you pitch your voice. If you say **unjani?** with a high note on the "u," it means "How are you?" A low note on the "u" means "How are they?"

Speak Zulu!

Sawubona. Unjani?	Hello, how are you?
Ngikhona ngiyabonga	I'm fine, thanks
Igama lami ngu Lucky. Ngubani igama lakho?	My name is Lucky. What are you called?
Igama lami ngu Emma. Sizobonana kusasa	I'm Emma. See you tomorrow
Kuhle kakhulu! Hamba kahle	Great! Goodbye

Language matters

Like Swahili, the beginning of Zulu nouns shows you whether they are singular or plural. **Ogogo**, for instance, is "grandmother," **Ugogo** means "grandmothers."

Standard Zulu is taught in schools, and is also called Deep Zulu. People living in cities usually speak Urban Zulu, with many new words taken from English. They call a mobile phone **icell**, whereas in standard Zulu it is **umakhalekhukhwini**.

49

Quechua

Quechua-speaking countries

 Argentina

 Bolivia

 Chile

 Ecuador

 Peru

A short history of Quechua

Quechua was the language of the Inca Empire. When Spanish conquistadores first encountered the Inca in the early 16th century, their empire stretched down the western coast of South America from the equator to present-day Chile. Quechua was not written down until after the Spanish conquest, but the Inca used *quipu*, made of different colored cords, to make calculations and keep records.

Because of its importance in the region, Quechua was quickly studied and written down by missionaries, making it one of the earliest recorded South American languages. Today, Quechua is recognized as an official language in Peru, Bolivia and Ecuador.

Where is it spoken?

Quechua is spoken as a first language by about **9 million** people in South America.

Greetings

Rimaykullayki	Hello
Tupananchikkama	Goodbye
Pedroqa sutiymi…	My name is…
¿Allillanchu?	How are you?
Allillanmi	I'm fine
Mana allinmi kachkani	I'm not feeling well

Numbers

1	uk	6	suhta
2	iskay	7	qanchis
3	kimsa	8	pusah
4	tawa	9	hiskun
5	phiska	10	chunka

Pronunciation points

a	is pronounced like "a" in "father"
i	is pronounced like "ee" in "see"
y	is also pronounced like "ee" in "see"
ch	is pronounced like "ch" in "cheese"
p'	This sound is made by closing the vocal cords as the sound is pronounced. There is no English equivalent.
q	is pronounced as a deep "k" as in "card"
ll	is pronounced like "ly" in "million"

Speak Quechua!

Rimaykullayki. ¿Allillanchu?
Hello, how are you?

Allillanmi, solpayki
I'm fine, thanks

Pedroqa sutiymi. ¿Imataq sutiyki?
My name is Pedro. What is yours?

Mariaqa sutiymi. Paqarinkama
I'm Maria. See you tomorrow

¡Allin p'unchay kachun!
Have a nice day!

Language matters

Quechua has contributed many words to the English language: **alpaca**, **coca**, **condor**, **guano**, **jerky** (jerked meat), **llama**, **puma**, **quinine** and many others. The name of the language in Quechua, **Runa Simi**, means simply "human speech."

51

Aa Ee CHch CHHchh Ee Hh Ii Kk KHkh K'k' Ll LIl Mm Nn ññ Oo Pp PHph P'p' Qq QHqh Q'q' Rr Ss SHsh Tt Uu Ww Yy
a e cha chha e ha i ka kha k'a la lla ma na ña o pa pî p'a qa qha q'a ra sa sha ta u wa ya

Mandarin Chinese

普通話
(Pǔtōnghuà)

Mandarin-speaking countries

 China

 Taiwan

A short history of Mandarin Chinese

The ancestor of today's Mandarin goes back 1,500 years. It was originally spoken in the north of China on the plains around Beijing.

Mandarin Chinese became important in the 19th century, when it was the language spoken in the court of the Chinese emperor. But it was only one of many Chinese languages.

Until the middle of the 20th century most Chinese people spoke only their local language. That changed when all Chinese schools began to teach Mandarin. Chinese is also spoken by large Chinese communities around the world, although many overseas Chinese speak Cantonese, a dialect of Mandarin.

China

Taiwan

Where is it spoken?

Mandarin Chinese is spoken by over **a billion people** worldwide.

Greetings

nǐ hǎo	Hello
zàijiàn	Goodbye
wǒ jiào...	My name is…
nǐ zěnmeyàng?	How are you doing?
hái bú cuò, xièxie	I'm fine, thank you
wǒ bù shūfu	Not so good

Numbers

1	**yī**	6	**liù**
2	**èr**	7	**qī**
3	**sān**	8	**bā**
4	**sì**	9	**jiǔ**
5	**wǔ**	10	**shí**

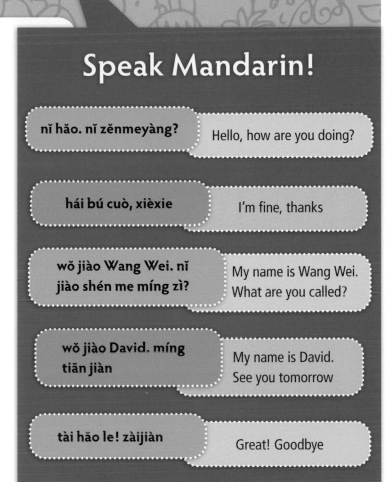

Speak Mandarin!

nǐ hǎo. nǐ zěnmeyàng? — Hello, how are you doing?

hái bú cuò, xièxie — I'm fine, thanks

wǒ jiào Wang Wei. nǐ jiào shén me míng zì? — My name is Wang Wei. What are you called?

wǒ jiào David. míng tiān jiàn — My name is David. See you tomorrow

tài hǎo le! zàijiàn — Great! Goodbye

Pronunciation points

Mandarin is a tonal language, meaning vowels can have different musical sounds or tones. There are four basic tones and a fifth neutral tone. The marks above the vowel tell you which tone to use.

ī — in a word like **yī** is the first tone – the high level tone – like singing a musical note

ó — in **tóu** is the second tone – the rising tone – your voice starts low and goes up

ǎ — in **hǎo** is the third or falling-rising tone. It goes down, then up

è — in **èr** is a falling tone. It falls in pitch from high to low

a — Any vowel without an accent is a neutral tone. It is toneless and pronounced weakly.

This pitch or intonation in which a sound is spoken affects the meaning. **Tāng** with a high tone means "soup," but **táng** with a rising tone means "sugar."

Language matters

You can make questions by adding **ma** (neutral tone) to the end of a sentence: **chī bǎo le ma?** means "Have you eaten?"

There are two ways of writing Chinese. The traditional way of writing the language is in characters. It's beautiful and fascinating, but hard work to learn. There are more than 2,000 separate characters. The script that uses the same letters as English is called Pinyin. It only has capital letters for place names and people's names, not at the beginning of sentences.

Aa Bb Cc Dd Ee Ff Gg Hh Ii Jj Kk Ll Mm Nn Oo Pp Qq Rr Ss Tt Uu Vv Ww Xx Yy Zz
a be ce de e ef ge ha i jie ke el em ne o pe qiu ar es te u ve wa xi ya ze

53

Nonverbal languages

Nonverbal communication doesn't use spoken words, but finds other ways to transmit information via visual signals or sounds. Nonverbal languages have developed when spoken languages cannot be heard or understood.

Smoke signals

Before the invention of telephones and satellite communication, humans needed to be able to send messages over long distances. Smoke signals were an effective way of transmitting warnings of enemy attacks or gathering people to an agreed meeting place.

Native Americans are historically known for their use of smoke signals. The ancient Chinese also used them to communicate over long distances, from one tower to the next, along the Great Wall of China.

Drumming

Drumming is another way of transmitting messages over long distances. The talking drum is an hourglass-shaped drum from West Africa. Its pitch can be changed to mimic human speech. An African drum message can be transmitted at a speed of 100 miles (160 kilometers) an hour.

Whistling

Whistling languages developed in places with very rugged terrain where shepherds and farmers needed to keep in touch with one another across the steep valleys. Silba is the name of one of these languages, which is still used in Gomera, one of the smaller Canary Islands. The language contains 4,000 words.

Computer codes

Computer programmers use special languages to make computers respond to our commands. They use codes, such as the binary code. The binary code shows words, numbers and instructions by using only the symbols 0 and 1. The binary code is also used in digital sound to make CDs and in the Braille alphabet, which makes it possible for blind people to read books by using their sense of touch.

Sign language

There are some signs that we all use instead of words. Thumbs-up or thumbs-down, high fives, or holding our noses, the gestures say it all; no words are needed. People who cannot hear or speak have created complete languages based on signs. They use their hands and fingers, facial expressions and movements of the body to say everything that a spoken language can communicate.

Most countries have their own sign languages, just as they have their own spoken languages. The most widely used sign language in Canada and the USA is ASL (American Sign Language). Historically overlooked, BASL (Black American Sign Language) is gaining recognition.

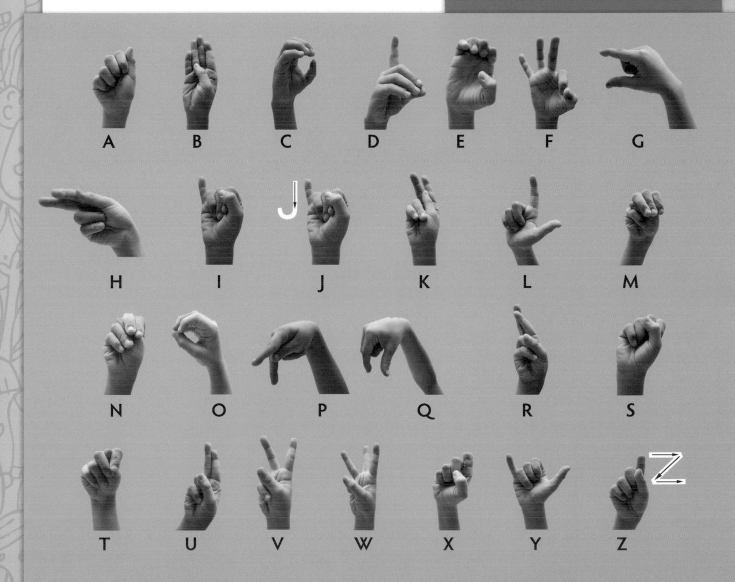

Semaphore

Semaphore is another way of sending messages across a long distance. Originally it was a system of sending signals at sea, by hoisting flags to the top of a ship's mast. During the 19th century a more sophisticated type of semaphore was developed. A person holds two colored flags, one in each hand. He or she can show different letters of the alphabet and numbers by changing the position of the flags.

Semaphore flags used at sea are red and yellow, but on land they are blue and white. However, semaphore isn't any good for sending secret messages because everyone can see it!

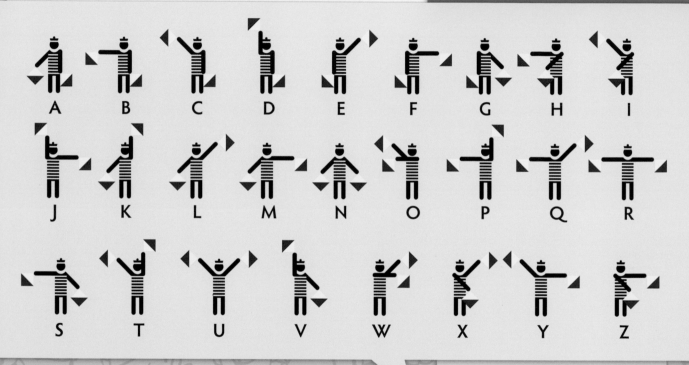

Can you understand this message?

Numbers

1		6	
2		7	
3		8	
4		9	
5		10	

It says: Lend me a phone

Morse code

_-- --- .-. ... ._. ...._

In 1830, an American inventor called Samuel Morse made a machine that used electrical signals to send messages along a wire. It was called the telegraph and it completely changed long-distance communication. You could send messages much further and much more quickly than ever before. Morse also invented a code for signaling different letters and numbers. Known as Morse code, it uses combinations of dots, spaces and dashes, which an operator taps out on a "straight key" (see photograph). If the person who receives the message knows Morse code, he or she can decode the message and work out what it means.

The most famous message is dot-dot-dot, dash-dash-dash, dot-dot-dot. The three letters are SOS, which stand for "Save Our Souls." It is a sign that you are in trouble and need help.

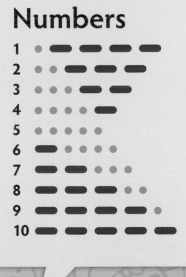

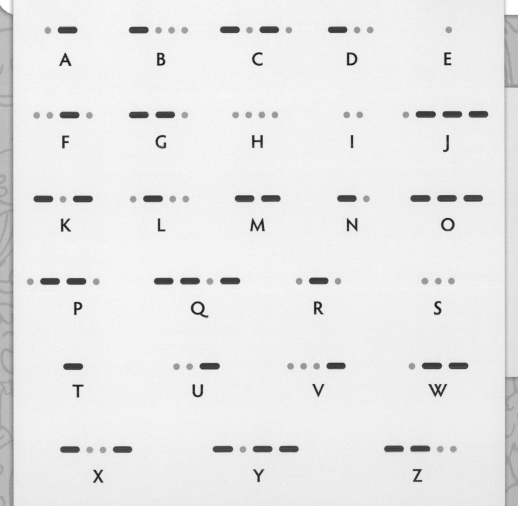

Numbers

1	·▬▬▬▬
2	··▬▬▬
3	···▬▬
4	····▬
5	·····
6	▬····
7	▬▬···
8	▬▬▬··
9	▬▬▬▬·
10	▬▬▬▬▬

Animal communication

Animals have many different ways of communicating, although none of them are as complex as human language. Some animals, like dogs and horses, learn to respond to words that we use for commands, but animals aren't able to learn to speak our language because their larynxes (voice boxes) are different.

Bee "waggle dance"

Honeybees seem to be able to tell other bees about new flowers that they have discovered. When they return to the hive, they do a kind of dance, which has been called a waggle dance. They dance around, following a figure-of-eight pattern, waggling their bodies. The direction and the length of the dance shows where and how far away the flower is. The bees use the sun as a point of reference. If the flower is in the direction of the sun, they perform their dance straight up the walls of the hive.

Whale song

Some species of whales, but not all of them, use sound to communicate. The humpback whale makes noises that are similar to human music. We don't know whether the whales are really singing. The sounds are only made during the mating season, so they may be performed to attract a partner.

Caribbean reef squid

These small squid are able to change the color patterns on their bodies. They use this ability to send messages and signals to other squid. They can send different messages at the same time by showing a variety of colors on different sides of their bodies. They use these signals to show whether they are interested or not in mating with another squid.

Dogs

Barking is the most obvious way in which dogs communicate. It might show that they are concerned about an intruder. Short, sharp barks are more likely to show pleasure, as when they think they're going to be taken for a walk. They also use their tails to show their mood. When the tail is held high, it shows that the dog is alert and aware; the tail between the legs means that the dog is afraid. Dogs wag their tails if they're uncertain about their environment, when they're excited and sometimes as a signal of aggression.

Birdsong

Birds make short, sharp calls, usually as a warning to other birds that they have seen a cat or some other predator. They also make a longer string of noises, called "birdsong." These are often long, complex and enjoyable to listen to, like music. Some birds are very good mimics and include the sounds that they hear around them. The lyrebird (above) lives in the rain forests of Australia and can imitate other birds and animals, and even chainsaws.

Glossary

Articles These are words like **a**, **an** and **the**. **A** and **an** are called **indefinite articles** and **the** is a definite article. Most languages have their own versions of articles. They go with nouns, usually in front of them.

Dialect This is a version of a language that is spoken in a particular area or by a particular group of people. It usually has a different accent and sometimes different vocabulary from the main language.

Grammar This is the way that words in a language are put together. The grammar of each language has its own set of rules. If you break them, it's called "bad grammar." One rule of English grammar is that adjectives come in front of nouns, so you say "a good child," not "a child good."

Mother tongue This is the first language that a child learns. In many countries, it may not be the language a person uses most regularly when they grow up.

Nouns These are the "naming words" in a language. They can refer to a thing, a person or a place. In many languages, but not English, all nouns have genders. Even things like tables and fields are either masculine or feminine. Some languages also have neuter nouns.

Object The object of a verb has the action done to it. The object can be a person, like "her," or a thing, like "tree": **I like her. We cut down the tree.**

Official language This is the language recognized by a country's law and that must be used for certain government functions. Sometimes there is more than one official language in any one country.

Script This is the way in which a language is written. Many European languages are written in the Roman or Latin alphabet. Scripts such as Arabic and Hebrew are read from right to left. Some scripts, such as Mandarin Chinese, are not based on letters but on little pictures, called characters, which can stand for whole words or ideas.

Subject This is the person who does the action the verb describes. **I am happy. She likes football.** The subject can also be a thing: **My car is green.**

Tones All languages have their own music. To ask a question in English, for instance, you have to change the tone of your voice. Some languages, such as Chinese and Zulu, are called **tonal**. This means that words, or even parts of words, have a particular music, or tone. If you get it wrong, you may change the meaning of a word completely.

Verbs These are "doing words." They describe an action, like **run**, **make**, **buy**. They can also describe a state, like **is**, **are**, **feel**. Verbs can have subjects and objects.

Vocabulary This refers to all the individual words in a language. You can describe a person as "having a good vocabulary" if he or she knows lots of words.

Index

Say "Goodbye" in 48

Ukudigada
Aleut-Eskimo

Tavauvutit
Inuktitut

Hej hej
Danish

Goodbye
English

Tot ziens
Dutch

Ekosi
Cree

Iame
Innu

Hwyl fawr
Welsh

Tokša akhé
Lakota

Au revoir
French

Giga-waabamin minawaa
Anishinabe

Agur
Basque

Hágóone'
Navajo

Atiu
Mi'kmaq

Adiós
Spanish

Arrivederci
Italian

Chi pisa lachike
Choctaw

Nimitsittas
Nahuatl

Orevwa
Haitian Creole

Ch'abej chik
K'iche'

Adeus
Portuguese

Tupananchikkama
Quechua

Salapo ciwa
Umbundu

Jajuechapeve
Guaraní

Tot siens
Afrikaans

Goodbye!

different languages

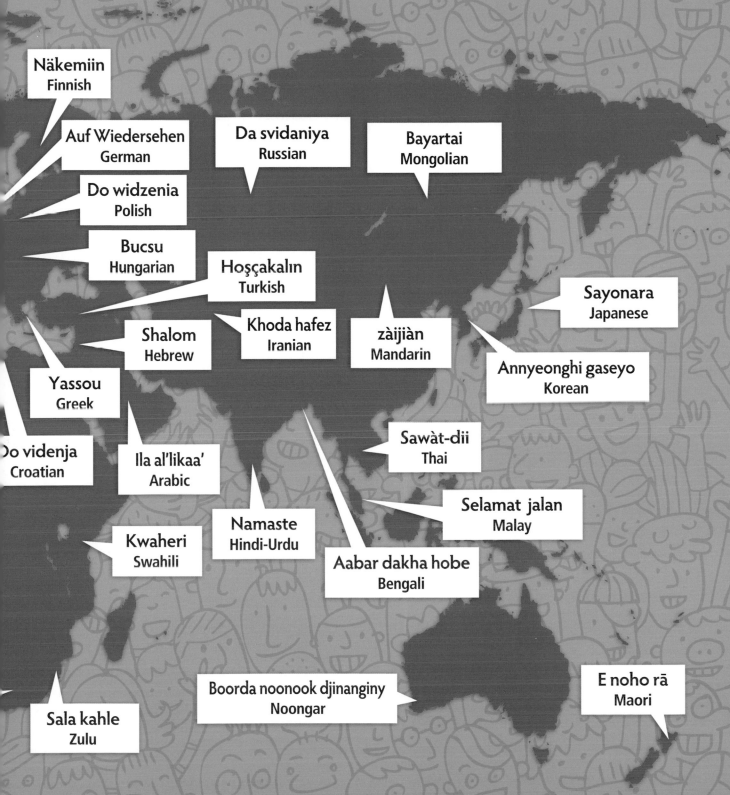

Näkemiin
Finnish

Auf Wiedersehen
German

Do widzenia
Polish

Bucsu
Hungarian

Da svidaniya
Russian

Bayartai
Mongolian

Hoşçakalın
Turkish

Khoda hafez
Iranian

zàijiàn
Mandarin

Sayonara
Japanese

Shalom
Hebrew

Annyeonghi gaseyo
Korean

Yassou
Greek

Do videnja
Croatian

Ila al'likaa'
Arabic

Sawàt-dii
Thai

Namaste
Hindi-Urdu

Selamat jalan
Malay

Kwaheri
Swahili

Aabar dakha hobe
Bengali

Sala kahle
Zulu

Boorda noonook djinanginy
Noongar

E noho rā
Maori